Praise for
Discover t

"Many companies talk about delivering customer service, but Bob has always delivered service at a much higher consistent level through the "Black Tie Customer Experience." He separates himself from the rest with his delivery and the way he shares his knowledge in writing so others can gain that advantage of "Hospitality"—the secret sauce to not only satisfying your clients but also having them anxious to utilize your services over and over again!

—Timothy A. Dimoff,
chief executive officer, president,
SACS Consulting and
Investigative Services, Inc.

"Bob's *25 Ways to Deliver Black Tie Hospitability* is a must-read for anyone who wants to take themselves or their team from a culture of customer service to a culture of true hospitality!"

—Bart Burger, managing director,
educational services,
Bowling Proprietors' Association of America

"The concepts in this book apply to any business and any industry. I've been so fortunate to know and work with Bob for over ten years. I've seen him in action applying his Black Tie Concepts and have witnessed good events turn into extraordinary events. Using and applying Bob's concepts and Black Tie Takeaways can help any business strengthen its brand and build and maintain a loyal, devoted customer base. Incorporating his principles has helped me develop and train a staff dedicated to cultivating exceptional guest experiences. I encourage any business leader to take the time to read this book, apply the Black Tie Concepts, and watch your business transform."

—Stephanie Monastra, director,
Conference Center,
Kent State University at Stark

"Bob's unique insight about what really matters in any service industry is crucial to setting you apart from others. His career has made him the expert of experts, and I learn something new with every chapter! To read this book and not apply it to your business and life should be a crime!"

—Bob Pontius, regional director
of business development,
Danbury Senior Living

"Divine Events has contracted with Bob several times. His customer service excellence program made a huge impact on our team and level of service. We've also had a few refresher sessions with the group over the last three years. The topics were timely, on target, and appropriate to grow our team's expertise in serving our clients, from private events to our largest customer event of 8,000. We produce approximately 2000 events per year, and our team needs these sessions to "stay on top of our game." Bob and his program have helped us improve our level of service and have been instrumental in our ability to grow our business and our team."

—Pam Howatt, owner and founder,
Divine Events

"Sometimes a book comes along that simply changes everything—and here it is! You grow your business by connecting with your customers; that is the Power of Hospitality. Bob has taken his years of successfully transforming businesses, organizations, and nonprofits and boiled down effective strategies to simple but profound success principles that all of us need to win. You'd be wise to have your team read and apply this book—before your competition does!"

—Tom Jones, president,
Legacy Senior Benefits

Missing Link

25 Ways
to Delight Customers
with **Black Tie Hospitality**

Bob Pacanovsky

Discover The Missing Link
25 Ways to Delight Customers with Black Tie Hospitality

First edition. 2023

ISBN 979-8-9879198-0-4 (paperback)
        979-8-9879198-1-1 (ebook)
Printed in the United States of America

Requests to publish work from this book or to schedule the author for an event, contact:
Bob Pacanovsky
Bob@BobPacanovsky.com
www.BobPacanovsky.com
(330) 352-6084

Acknowledgments

This book has been a journey for me, one I thought would never evolve into writing a page to say Thank You.

I started this process about five years ago and started writing not one, but two books, except they're still not finished. I'm not sure what changed in my mind with this book, but I do know that the people below had something to do with it.

So I give thanks to:

- Gail Kerzner, my editor. Thank you for being more patient with me than you should have been throughout these years. More importantly, thank you for your guidance and expertise in getting this book published.

- Tom Jones. Thanks for being that extra set of eyes for me when it came to talking about the different chapters of the book. You made me see things from different points of view, and I greatly appreciate that.

- My NSA Family. Seven years ago, I didn't even know there was an organization called the National Speakers Association. Since then, I've been blessed to meet and work with so many professionals who have given me valuable advice and constructive criticism. But I have to single out a handful: Mj Callaway, Jeff Koziatek, and Peter Margaritis.

Thank you for going above and beyond to help me become a better speaker.

- The teams I've been blessed to hire and work with over the years. Thank you for embracing the teachings and becoming the best professionals one could ever work with! You made our companies and brand what they were.

- My clients. Thank you for the opportunity and confidence to work with you and your audiences. I hope my message has made an impact, and I appreciate your friendship. And a special thank you goes to Jarrod Clabaugh for not only writing the Foreword of this book but also for becoming a good friend in just a few short years.

- Finally, and most importantly, the last sentence people read in my Introduction before I walk on any stage is: "However, he is most proud of being married to his wife, Connie, for 32 years and his son, Adam." I mean that. Thank you for all your support, wisdom, faith, and love. I'm not where I am without both of you.

Contents

....

(🎀) HOSPITALITY IS...

Foreword

Within the pages of this book, readers will discover valuable insights Bob has learned over his career in hospitality that will help them nurture their own good-will in a manner to best serve others as Bob does: as a true servant leader. His focused, genuine character shines through in the hospitality he practices daily.

This book provides its readers with actionable and applicable lessons, whether it's providing someone with something invisible that absolutely makes them feel seen or by applying genuine, thoughtful behaviors that enrich others' lives. I have known Bob for many years, and he lives the lessons he shares within this book's pages. People genuinely value their interactions with him because he places his clients, his peers, and his friends at the center of his hospitable practices. No one walks away from Bob wondering if he was being sincere or was listening to them. His is a guiding vision, and he carefully and methodically explains much of it right here.

His everyday habits have transformed many people simply because it feels good to make others feel good. These behaviors harken back to the old Golden Rule of treating others as you wish to be treated. Bob's sheer delight and unmatched skill in bringing compassionate and targeted "wow" experiences to those with whom he interacts are lessons from which we can all benefit.

Bob uses his insights to remind us that making people feel valued and respected doesn't take much. But it does take practice and a focused mindset to shift from our current culture of "deliver it fast without care" to "deliver it with care to continue that practice."

When applying the skills outlined within these pages, it becomes quite clear to the reader that Bob understands better than most the value of hospitality and the need to build personal connections among one another. Our culture has shifted to caring only about immediacy so quickly that we've shattered the true need to build connections and lift one another up through friendship, fellowship, and focus.

The lessons in this book will improve the hospitality you provide while also ensuring that you craft relationships that lead to unwavering connections. In fact, these lessons make Bob the authority on true servant leadership and hospitality—the perfect kind of leader from whom we can all learn.

Jarrod A. Clabaugh
Certified Association Executive (CAE)
President & CEO,
Ohio Society of Association Professionals

Introduction

Why a Book on Hospitality?

The last few years (2020-2022) have been most challenging for many of us. And as we were starting to come out of the pandemic, I noticed something missing regarding this concept we call "Customer Service." I wasn't the only one. As I talked to people at the conferences and events where I spoke, they noticed it too, as it seemed to get a little more frustrating to be a customer or an employee.

What was the missing link? Yes, I believe it was customer service at times, but it was more than that. It was the Power of Hospitality and how we were making our customers and prospects *feel* while we were serving, leading, or interacting with them.

At the beginning of 2022, an idea popped into my head. What if I came up with 22 ways to show Hospitality in 2022? As I came up with the list, I realized they were all ideas I've talked about or currently talk about as a speaker and trainer in my keynotes and workshops.

I created the list, put it out as a PDF, and posted it on my social media channels. The response was better than I expected. Some people asked me to send them the list so they could use it for their staff meetings.

The PDF then morphed into a new Black Tie Hospitality Video Series, which was also well received. But I wanted to take it a few steps further. What you're about to read are those extra steps. And since we are not in 2022 any longer, it didn't make sense to me to keep these concepts at 22. So I decided to add three more to make it a total of twenty-five.

This book is an easy read, with short chapters—no more than two or three pages. And it focuses on how to make Hospitality an everyday habit for your organization. Hopefully, these concepts will resonate with you and your people. And if I can make you think and act differently about how we make others feel, how we should focus on connecting with them, engaging them, building trust with them, appreciating them, and every once in a while giving them a WOW experience, I've done my job.

I'm not finished, however. At the end of each chapter will be a quick summary of that particular idea and how you can turn it into a Black Tie Takeaway. Look for this symbol at the end of each chapter.

What would your business look like if you implemented these 25 Takeaways? You will then have discovered the Missing Link.

I believe Customer Service can *bring people into* your business. But Hospitality? That will *bring them back.*

⊛ HOSPITALITY IS...

1

The art of making that personal connection.

....

What's your definition of Hospitality? Some people say "friendly" or welcoming." Others may think of the hospitality industry, and they think of hotels, restaurants, food, and venues. While there may be numerous definitions of Hospitality, the one that strikes me the most is: "The art of making a personal connection between you and someone else." Let that sink in, and read it again. "The art of making a personal connection between you and someone else."

It's not always easy to practice Hospitality today in our culture, is it? We live and work in what some say is an "inhospitable world" based on how people look, act, and speak to others. People are tired, stressed, and perhaps improperly trained. Companies are short-staffed and trying to survive. Technology sometimes takes the place of humans. And the one thing we sometimes forget is how to treat and care for each other.

This is why we need to strive to make these personal/ emotional connections, to build relationships, and to be kinder and nicer to people. Yes, we need to do this even if we're just stopping into a store to buy one or two items. Don't you feel a little better if the employee welcomes you, asks how your day is going, and thanks you for coming in? In those brief minutes, that is Hospitality.

You can feel something different when someone shows you Hospitality, can't you? Maybe they're making you feel more appreciated by just doing the little things to make you feel like a VIP, not like a number. Maybe they'll say "Thank you," whether by a note, email, text, or call. Whatever the means, chances are you'll remember those gestures. That's making a personal connection because they're making it about you. Just think if we experienced this and delivered this every day!

Competition in business today is at an all-time high. While we should always have a quality product or service, that is becoming a commodity. I can get it almost anywhere. What separates your product or service from everyone else is your people and how they will take care of customers through the entire customer experience. It starts with—and continues with—showing and delivering hospitality, connecting with people to make them feel something different about the experience they're getting with your organization. This may be the difference between "one and done" and building that loyalty which can increase retention, engagement, and revenue for your organization.

BLACK TIE TAKEAWAY

What's one thing you can do today to make that personal connection with someone, whether they're a customer, guest, prospect, or employee?

_____

_____

_____

_____

(⊷) HOSPITALITY IS...

2

Knowing what business you're in.

I'm sure you know what business you're in. You're living it every day. So why do I ask people in my seminars and workshops to write out their answers to the question, "What business are you in"? They know the answer — or do they?

The answers I receive vary based on the audience—responses such as "customer service," "entertainment," "logistics," "caring for others," and "people." I tell them their answers are all correct, and then I give them my answer. This answer turned our business around because we were able to change the focus and mind-set of how we treated our customers and employees.

We're all in the Hospitality Business first, providing whatever you do. Being in the Hospitality Business means we're all in the People Business, first and foremost. Starbucks tells its people, "We are not in the Coffee Business serving People but in the People Business serving Coffee."

"But Bob," you may ask, "isn't that what Customer Service is?" Yes, and no.

I believe Customer Service is task-oriented. It's those things we should be doing anyway.

- *Being friendly*
- *Greeting people*
- *Making sure of our promises*
- *Returning calls/emails on a timely basis*

Hospitality is how we make our customers and prospects feel while we're doing those tasks.

Customer Service can bring customers into your business. We need to provide service for our business to survive. But if you just provide Customer Service, I believe you're in the sales business. There's nothing wrong with this; new customers are always good for any business. But how many customers are you retaining? Or are they churning out of your business? Yes, you're doing some good things for them, but something is missing—that missing link, that spark, that feeling. And let's face it! No one remembers ordinary service.

Providing Hospitality. That brings your customers back—and more! With Hospitality, you're in the marketing business. Because of the way you're treating your customers and making them feel, they now have the opportunity to market your business for you through their word of mouth and their storytelling.

We all know this is the best way to bring in more customers, but we may not commit to providing Hospitality.

BLACK TIE TAKEAWAY

What about you and your organization? Does everyone know you're in the hospitality—the people—business first? While we all know this, are you practicing it and carrying it out?

_____

_____

_____

_____

⊶ HOSPITALITY IS...

3

Understanding it's not just a uniform.

Our company started in the events and catering business serving people. And business was "okay," but something was missing: a mindset on how to treat our customers and move them to the loyal-and-repeat stage for our company.

The change came about in two ways for us. We started focusing on being in the hospitality business, creating memories for our guests, rather than in the event and catering business serving people. Second, we created a training program that focused on how we trained and treated our people so they could serve and wow our customers at the highest level possible. That's how the Black Tie mindset—and now the brand of my speaking and training company—came about.

The black tie was a part of the uniform for our staff. You see, I had the best staff around. I know I'm biased when I say that, but I absolutely believe that. For close to fifteen years, many people wore that black tie and the rest of the uniform for the events and catering company that bore my name. They wore the tie along with the white tux shirt, black vest, and black pants. While I realize this might have been a "standard uniform" for our industry at the time, when they put it on, they transformed into "Event Super Heroes." This didn't happen overnight, however.

Before they could put on that uniform and step onto any event floor we worked on (and we worked at some of the classiest venues, businesses, and homes in our area), they first had to learn what the Black Tie Mentality was all about. This was an eight-hour training program followed by mentoring and coaching once they started working on these event floors. Oh, and I should mention that almost everyone who worked for us did so on a part-time, as-needed basis. That meant working only a few times a month in a job that was both physically and mentally demanding.

Why did they do it? Some needed extra income, others needed to fill time on their schedule, and some wanted to work at some really cool venues. Actually, I think this was a big reason for many of them, myself included. But I also knew if we were going to make an impact and have the opportunity for repeat and loyal customers and venues, I needed to create a training program that separated us from everyone else and gave our people the chance to go above and beyond—to that "Black Tie" level—when it came to serving, acting, leading, and communicating.

And they responded. These people became our "Black Tie Super Heroes" and helped this small company in Akron, Ohio, create over 7,000 events, meetings, and receptions in fifteen years. They helped this company work at major venues throughout northeast Ohio, including attractions like Stan Hywet Hall & Gardens, The National Inventors Hall of Fame, The Crawford Auto & Aviation Museum, The International Soap Box Derby, Gervasi Vineyard, and The Pro Football Hall of Fame (plus many others).

Speaking of the Pro Football Hall of Fame, they helped this company cater twenty-five Induction Parties for the players in five years. No other company, some of which were much larger than we were, even came close. And they helped this company secure numerous repeat and loyal clients, some of whom were with us for ten, twelve, or even fourteen years straight, leading to a profitable company for almost all of these fifteen years.

I credit all of this to their passion, tremendous work ethic, and willingness to always go above and beyond when working with our customers and guests as well as their understanding, practicing, and implementing of Black Tie Hospitality every day, at every event.

BLACK TIE TAKEAWAY

What's "your uniform" or mindset when investing and training the people in your organization? Can it be improved, revised, or changed to create a "Black Tie" mentality when serving your customers?

_____

_____

_____

_____

⊙ HOSPITALITY IS...

4

Something invisible that can make a memorable impact.

It's not easy, but it happens all the time. Hospitality is something you can *feel*. You may not be able to see it, but you know it's there.

Again, I need to give some big props again to our staff at our event/catering company. Yes, we trained them to show Hospitality, but they really took it to the next level.

I heard all the time from clients about them—not just that they were nice and friendly (which they were), but also that they would strive to achieve that "Black Tie" Level of Service to be helpful and pitch in to do whatever our clients needed. They would see a guest who had a question and would stop what they were doing to help them find an answer.

They were passionate about serving our clients and guests at the events. They knew we had only one opportunity to make them feel special, and they always looked for ways to do that.

Finally, here's one of the best compliments I've ever received about them (and I heard this numerous times): "Bob, your staff is invisible! They're so seamless with their service, and I haven't had to worry about anything the entire night!"

Hospitality is something you can feel. You may not be able to see it, but you know it's there. Do your clients know it's there by how your staff is treating them, serving them, and making them feel something that will make them a storyteller for your company?

BLACK TIE TAKEAWAY

How about your team? Are they invisible when they're serving your customers?

If they're invisible, this usually means they're taking care of your customers' needs, and that's always good!

_____

_____

_____

_____

⬖ HOSPITALITY IS...

5

A history lesson we can all use.

....

In today's economy, we always need to look forward and stay innovative and creative for our organizations and our clients.

However, we should look at history on occasion to see where we've come from and how things were done in the past. I was happy to discover some history I believe is still needed in our business world today when it comes to Hospitality.

Below you'll see two Greek words. Unless you're a student of languages, you probably won't be able to decipher their meanings. I wasn't able to either.

The first word is Philao. **Φιλό**

The second word is Xenos. **ξενος**

They mean "Loving or Welcoming Strangers."

Isn't that what we're supposed to do every day in our organizations? And then turning those strangers into people who like, trust, and respect us because of how we treat them?

What's your strategy for loving or welcoming strangers? Do you onboard your employees and customers and not only welcome them but also make them feel comfortable and able to solve any of their challenges?

If so, you're well on your way to taking care of your people and ensuring loyalty and long-term business simply by reliving history.

BLACK TIE TAKEAWAY

Are you reliving history every day by how your staff welcomes people in your organization? Whether they're a customer, prospect, employee, vendor, or community member, you should treat them equally and show them a consistent history lesson.

_____

_____

_____

(⊶) HOSPITALITY IS...

6

Doing the little things to make customers feel more valued.

Legendary college basketball coach John Wooden said, "It's the little details that are vital. Little things make big things happen." Hospitality is taking care of those little details for your customers. Maybe it's that call or text to let them know their product is on the way or that the delivery is running a little late, and they didn't want to worry you.

Or maybe it's that phone call, saying "Thank You for your business, and here's my number if you have any challenges with our company."

Or maybe it's going "above and beyond" with a small gesture, a card, thank you, or something meaningful for them that will make them *feel* better.

What is it for you? What are those little things you do that are vital to the overall customer experience?

When you perfect these "little things" (which really aren't that little), everything your organization does now becomes better in the eyes of your customer or prospect.

In our companies, we had the "big things down." We had wonderful food, and our service was outstanding. But this was true for many other companies, most of which were bigger than we were. I told my staff if we were going to be successful and have clients return to us to book more events, we needed to make sure that the "little things" we did—before, during (especially at this time), and after the event—were critical to the overall success of the event. That would mean they always looked for ways to deliver that "Black Tie" level of service excellence and hospitality. This service could be how we greeted and spoke to clients, or maybe it was anticipating what they were looking for because we were able to read body language and their cues. Maybe this "Black Tie" level of service was remembering some details about the event, even minor ones, and being proactive so our clients didn't have to concern themselves with them.

I'll leave you with this thought: Customer Service is the task-oriented thing we should be doing—greeting people, returning calls, and taking care of orders and complaints.

Hospitality is how we make our customers *feel* when we're performing these tasks.

BLACK TIE TAKEAWAY

What are two or three "little things" you and the people in your organization can be doing to make your customers feel something positive about your organization that they might not have done in the past?

_____

_____

_____

_____

⊙ HOSPITALITY IS...

7

Asking for feedback on how you can improve their experience.

Are you old enough to remember the rotary phone and the answering machine?

Seems like ages ago, right?

Here's a brief story about these two ancient devices that made a significant impact on our business. By the way, I think there's a right way and a not-so-right way to ask for feedback.

I don't think the right way is to spend 14 minutes answering question after question on a survey from a company that wants my feedback on how they did. of course, they tell you it will only take "a few minutes." I don't think this is the right way, yet we see this time and time again.

When I first opened my restaurant in 1994, I knew I needed to set us apart from everyone else in our community. One of the ideas that worked really well for us was asking our customers for their feedback. But we did it by using these two devices.

A few times a month, we randomly selected 20-25 customers who had ordered from us the week before, and someone on our team called them in the evening. Now remember, in 1994 we didn't have caller ID, but we did have answering machines.

I wanted their feedback on their meal—if there was a part of it they liked (or didn't) and if someone from our staff was memorable.

The entire call took under two minutes, but the impact was priceless. Customers came back the following week shocked that a restaurant called them to ask for their feedback. They felt special.

And now I had data, and I used it to help improve our menu items and systems. We needed to look at recognizing staff for a great job—and more. If we did have a challenge with an order, I knew about it and could do something about it.

BLACK TIE TAKEAWAY

Can you select random customers to call, text, or email to ask for their feedback? Make it short and sweet (not 14 minutes), and then do something with the data because it's invaluable for your business.

HOSPITALITY IS...

8

Looking for ways to personalize the experience.

....

How do you feel as a customer when someone knows you, greets you by name, knows what you like and what you've ordered before? You feel pretty good, right?

I call it *The Art of Personalizing the Guest Experience.* As you know from me by now, Hospitality is the art of making a personal connection between you and someone else.

So personalizing the experience is right in the definition. How do we do this today with all the technology present and people's limited attention spans? Here are a few ideas:

- Be present. This means keeping your focus on your customers and their needs, not on the 45 other things you want to do at the same time.

- Doing this means you're listening to your customers. Remember, there's a difference between hearing them and actively listening to them.

- Doing this also means you're asking the right questions—for both your business and fun purposes. We need to know what's important to them about our product or service, but make it fun, too. Ask questions about their favorite beverage or sports team and the number of children they have.

- Doing this means you're paying attention to the details. You've heard this before, but it's worth repeating: the little details are vital for the customer experience. They help make the big things happen.

- And doing this can truly personalize the service you deliver to your clients.

And if you do all of these, you're on your way to creating loyal customers, those who become your best marketers and storytellers because they feel connected to your company—all due to the personal connection you've made.

All of this goes back to the first question I asked: How do you *feel* when someone makes it personal for you and makes you feel like you're a VIP, not just a number?

Do the same for your customers. That's creating a Hospitality experience.

BLACK TIE TAKEAWAY

How can you personalize the experience your customers receive when they work with your organization? Come up with one or two ways. Once you come up with those and they work, what are one or two more?

_____

_____

_____

_____

⬮ HOSPITALITY IS...

9

Giving people the right perception of you.

"Perception is 9/10ths of the law. How people perceive you usually becomes their truth."

This is one of my favorite sayings I used to tell all my staff. Unfortunately, it's even more true today in business because of our technology. What message are you and those you work with sending out by how you look, act, and speak?

Studies have shown that when we see a brand or person in the first seven to ten seconds, 11 major synapses are firing so quickly in our brains, we don't even realize it. They're either telling us to move forward or to be cautious with our next steps. Do people perceive you as a hospitable host?

Can you picture a beautiful lobby that's so shiny the floors are glistening because they're so clean? And you're drawn in by the appealing fragrance? Beautiful pictures adorn the walls, and lovely, colorful plants enhance the lobby.

And then . . . an employee greets you wearing a badly stained, wrinkled uniform. They don't acknowledge you because they're too busy being hypnotized by their phone, and when they do look up to greet you, they barely make eye contact with you and don't smile. *Now* what's your perception of that business? And can you see that you developed this perception in fewer than ten seconds?

This is the power of your mind.

So I told my staff this saying (which they named a "Robert J. ism" because I guess I said it often): "Perception is 9/10ths of the law. How people perceive us could become their truth." I also explained to them what it meant in our world, especially as guests would walk into the beautifully decorated ballrooms and event spaces we used to work in. The first impression and last impression of the event needed to come from us. We did this by making sure both our brand and our people knew how to look, act, and speak.

These impressions needed to be perfect, and we made sure we looked at the situation as if we were the guests, even if it was just for a few seconds.

BLACK TIE TAKEAWAY

How are you and your business perceived? Have you ever asked this question? There are two ways to find the answers besides reading it somewhere on social media: one, become a customer or prospect in your business, even for a few seconds, and two, ask someone who's already a customer. You'll find out a lot either way.

_____

_____

_____

_____

 **HOSPITALITY** IS...

10

Building peace of mind.

Zig Ziglar, the legendary motivational speaker, said, "If people like you, they'll listen to you, but if they trust you, they'll do business with you."

Trust is a powerful emotion and an outstanding character trait to possess. But how is trust related to Hospitality? I believe keeping your word and your promises builds both trust and peace of mind.

Maybe this image will help.

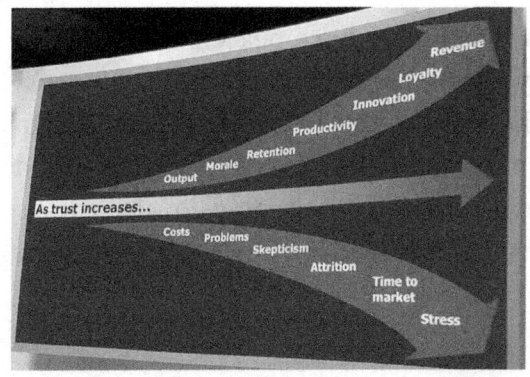

I took this picture when I was an audience member in 2017 when I attended the National Conference for the National Speakers Association, of which I'm still a member.

The speaker was from a company, The Trust Outlook, which studies, researches, and focuses on the principle of trust in the workplace. As trust increases in a customer relationship, look at what also increases: loyalty, retention, morale, and innovation, to name a few concepts.

I believe these come about because of how we treat our customers and make them feel more valued and appreciated. If you're taking care of them, their details, and their needs, you're lifting a tremendous weight from them.

You're telling and showing them their business and relationship is important to you, and you're delivering on your promises. What does all of this do? It builds peace of mind.

And once your customers have peace of mind about the business you're doing with them, and they trust you, guess what also starts to happen? They begin to become brand storytellers for your business and products, and they start to become loyal customers—all because you're creating powerful conditions of trust.

BLACK TIE TAKEAWAY

What are you doing to create conditions of trust with your clients? Do they trust you to take care of and solve their challenges?

_____

_____

_____

_____

(⚬) HOSPITALITY IS...

11

Putting yourself in their shoes.

....

I often ask in my seminars, "Would *YOU* do business with *YOU*?" I get answers such as, "Of course, Bob. Our business is fantastic." I hope that's the case all the time, but every once in a while, we need to change our thinking and *not* be a part of our business. We need to take off the blinders we put on and put ourselves in our customers' shoes.

This is an eye-opening exercise, and we need to do it even more, especially today. If you can put yourselves in your customers' shoes and their eyes and ears, you'll get to see, hear, touch, taste, and most importantly, feel what they do when they work with you and/ or your organization.

How do you know what's impacting your customers if you've never experienced problems such as long wait times and products no longer available in inventory?

This leads me to my next thought: How many of your staff have ever bought your own product or service, or for that matter, have gotten to experience what first-class, "Black Tie" Service is all about?

Yet our staff is on our front lines and expected to serve our customers at a very high level. And then we get upset when they don't. Maybe it's because they don't know what that high level is supposed to be, and they don't know what your customer is going through to purchase your product.

At the next employee meeting or training, consider switching roles. The staff becomes the customers, and the leadership serves them. And to make it even more powerful, have the staff practice some scenarios they've encountered from customers while working for your organization. Now they get to be on the other side to feel the anxiety, frustration—or hopefully joy—the customers experience while trying to do business with you. Once this happens, ideally, everyone will have a better understanding of what being a customer in your business is all about and how your employees can now make these customers feel by showing and giving them some Hospitality.

BLACK TIE TAKEAWAY

Take that step back away from your organization, and look at it one day a month as if you were a customer or prospect. Then have your employees do the same.

_____

_____

_____

_____

⊕ HOSPITALITY IS...

12

Being empowered to take care of the customer.

As a customer, how often do you hear these statements?

I can't do that. I don't know.
That's not my job.
You will need to call back, as I can't help you.
You'll have to talk to_____.

The list can go on and on.

The above statements don't sound like they're helpful, do they? How about your employees? Do you hear the same phrases from them?

We can change this, and I'll tell you the word that can be helpful: "empowered." Are your employees empowered to help customers?

Empowerment can happen if leadership is willing to give their people the tools, techniques, and training to help customers solve their challenges. That's why they're coming to your business, correct? There are pain points that need to be addressed.

The last thing a staff person needs is for somebody to be constantly looking over their shoulder to see if they're making a mistake, and frankly, that's the last thing a customer needs as well.

Have your people been trained and empowered to go "Black Tie" and use Hospitality to create that memorable experience? If so, fantastic! And keep doing it! If not, that's okay because you can take that step now. Remember, making someone *feel* they matter to you and you genuinely care about their experience with your organization is priceless. And that's what stories are made of.

BLACK TIE TAKEAWAY

If the words people in your organization say are somewhat negative, empower them to change the script and take ownership of your clients' needs.

_____

_____

_____

_____

(⊶) HOSPITALITY IS...

13

The culture of your organization.

....

If your staff feels welcomed, valued, and appreciated, so will your customers.

I believe before we can ever start serving our external customers, we must take care of those who come in every day, work long hours, work hard, and at times are the face of your company—your people.

Hospitality and Culture go hand in hand. Are we taking care of our people the right way? If we're going to take care of them, we need to have a solid culture based on hospitality—or welcome.

Think of it this way. Your culture is similar to the foundation of your building. For the building to be solid, you must first build and set the foundation. Otherwise, the building could weaken over time and start to crack.

Your culture is the same way. The question is, "How are you building your culture?" Are you creating a sense of welcome for your team? Is your work environment a place where they feel valued and appreciated? A place where their ideas matter, where they're empowered to not only do their jobs but also to make decisions that will benefit the customers?

I'm not sure if there's a magic formula for creating a solid culture that incorporates hospitality, but here's mine:

Vision + Core Values + Purpose + Mantra.

Vision
This comes from the leadership, and they should always communicate the vision to the team. If the team doesn't know where they're going, how can they do their jobs most effectively? What's the vision of your organization? And does everyone know it—and better yet, believe it?

Core Values
Once you have a vision, will you have the right people on your team with the right values to carry it out?

Core values come from your heart and soul, the values that drive you every day to do the very best you can. I believe we all have them, and it's the organization's job to find out what they are from their employees. Do these core values line up with your organization's values?

So ask your team to write down three of their core values. But here's the key. These words will be nouns, and your team will need to add an action verb in front of them to make them behavior-based. For example, if "trust" is a core value, what's the verb before it? It could be "I show trust by . . . " or "I build trust by . . . " Once you know a few of your team's core values, they become valuable to your culture. Seeing your team living out their core values in front of a customer is a perfect opportunity to acknowledge those values. This shows you recognize them.

Conversely, if your team isn't demonstrating their core values to customers or staff, you can show them how to do that, but always in private. This lets them know they need to improve because living out their core values is important to the organization and its culture.

Purpose

Everyone can describe "what they do." This is their job function. It's a little more challenging to answer why they do their job. That's their purpose.

For example, the function of a hotel housekeeper is to clean the room, change the sheets, etc. Their purpose could be: to provide a welcoming, clean, and safe environment so that each guest feels at home when they enter the room.

And the purpose of everyone on the team should tie into the purpose of the Organization. What's the purpose of your organization? My answer is "To attract and retain more customers and employees." We do this by providing a safe, clean, and welcoming environment, etc.

And once your team understands their purpose, it will affect how they perform their functions. organizations that have a solid purpose typically have a solid culture.

The last piece of the puzzle is your mantra, the internal mission statement of the organization for the employees. There might be one mantra for the entire company, or departments may have their own. But the key to your mantra and why it's essential for a solid culture is that the team members should have a say in creating it since they have to live it. Your mantra should be short and sweet—between three to ten words. Why? We can remember a phrase that simple. Here are some examples:

"We are Ladies and Gentlemen, serving Ladies and Gentlemen."

–Ritz Carlton

The most important customer is always in the room."

–Amazon

"Solving problems that others ignore" —Dyson

"Team . . . Easy . . . & WOW!
            —Robert J.—Events and Catering,
                    the company I founded

I'll leave you with this quote by Sir Richard Branson, founder of Virgin, which sums this up well: "Clients do not come first. Employees come first. If you take care of the employees, they will take care of the clients."

Build your culture (your foundation) on providing and showing Hospitality or welcome. Before you ever serve your customers, this foundation has to be solid because without your people, there's not much you can do.

BLACK TIE TAKEAWAY

At your next staff meeting, have everyone write out anonymously what they believe the culture is in your organization and/or department. You'll get a good idea of what everyone thinks is going on and how they feel while working in your organization.

⊶ HOSPITALITY IS...

14

The leadership in your organization.

....

What does leadership have to do with Hospitality? Isn't making that personal connection with others vital to being a leader? I'm sure you can think of a leader, supervisor, or boss you've worked with (or maybe still do) who isn't hospitable. How does it feel to be on the receiving end of that?

I don't know about you, but I don't have a degree in leadership. I'm not sure that's even a college major, but shouldn't it be? Students study many subjects and concepts, some of which are technical, while others may be more abstract. Nonetheless, we're not usually taught how to lead people, so we talk to people in leadership roles and maybe model our leadership style after them. Hopefully, these leadership traits stick with us.

At age 29, I became a "leader," and I thought I was good at it until I realized that I wasn't. And it cost me a lot.

Luckily, I found a few mentors who coached me and helped me see that being a leader involved many abilities, including utilizing influence, showing appreciation, holding employees accountable, and developing trust.

Colin Powell, the former secretary of state and four-star general, said, "Leadership comes down to creating conditions of trust. Good leaders serve selflessly, not self-serving." What's the difference between selfless and self-serving?

When someone is self-serving, it's all about them. They're doing what's necessary to make themselves look good first. They're often the first to take all the credit and the last to take all the blame. Serving selflessly is the opposite. It's all about your people. You want to make sure they get the credit first and the blame last. It's about putting their needs above yours, making sure they have all the tools to do their job and empowering them to do it. That's practicing Hospitality.

There's a term for this that many of us know: "servant leadership." Whichever of the two terms you use and follow—servant leadership or selfless leadership—doesn't matter. Following this mindset is important, especially today when people are starving for someone who will care, value, empower, and appreciate them.

BLACK TIE TAKEAWAY

I believe everyone in an organization can be a leader. You don't need a title or business card to show that. What's one thing you can do that will make you a better leader for yourself, the people you work with, and your organization?

_____

_____

_____

_____

⊙ HOSPITALITY IS...

15

Giving 2% more in appreciation.

....

Appreciation. Thankfulness. Gratitude.

I understand these words all mean the same, and we probably say and write them often. I hope you hear them from your clients often.

But I don't think we show enough appreciation, thankfulness, and gratitude to our clients, staff, and co-workers. If we did, they'd feel even more valued. So what's the deal then with giving 2% more? See, I don't think we have to mimic the phrase "Go big or go home" when it comes to appreciating and thanking people. I think it's the extra little things we do, that 2% that can make a big difference—like picking up the phone to say "Thank you for all your support." That's it. No sales pitch.

Try sending something in the mail they would ap-preciate, not one of your swag items. Or truly listen to them and get them their favorite bottle of wine or something from their favorite sports team or hobby. It doesn't have to cost a lot, but doing that 2% more separates you from everyone else.

For example:

I'm sure many of you show your appreciation to clients or employees by sending them a birthday card or email. That's a nice touch. Here's the 2% more: Send a card on the date they became a client (or employee). It could read, "Thanks for being a great client! Do you know it's been three years today since you became a part of our family? Thank you for your support. It means the world to us!"

Here's another 2% idea:

It was April 2021, and I was on my first flight back after COVID. I got home early on a Wednesday morning. At 8 am, I received an email from Delta Airlines, and the subject line read, "Thanks for flying with us." I'll be honest and say I thought it was going to be a long email survey asking, "How did we do?" Instead, this was the first sentence of an email I received from the VP of Flight Operations of Delta Airlines. "I want to personally thank you for trusting Delta with your first flight back."

They could have easily said, "Thank you for flying with us again," but they didn't. They did the extra 2% and found out it was my first flight back in over a year. They showed their appreciation and gratitude in just one sentence.

What have you done to give that extra 2% when showing appreciation to your people? Let me know; I'd love to hear about it. And if you need ideas, please reach out to me. I have plenty!

BLACK TIE TAKEAWAY

How do you give that 2% more? Write down an idea or two here of how you will show thankfulness and appreciation consistently.

_____

_____

_____

_____

(⊷) HOSPITALITY IS...

16

Always looking for ways to WOW!

....

I have a riddle for you. What's a word that has the same meaning whether it's spelled forwards and backwards, gives the feeling of something random or unexpected, *and* can create powerful stories about your product, your people, and your organization?

The answer is—WOW!

There's a reason why WOW means random and unexpected. If we were wowed all the time, experiences wouldn't have the same effect or significance. But when they're random and created with spectacular attention, they generate a wonderful feeling for our customers and hopefully for you, the person who delivered them.

Here's something to remember when it comes to the WOW factor. Your business should be in the *joy* business first; then add in the WOW. This means we should always be focusing on delivering joy to our customers. Because if they feel joy when they work with us, we're already creating positive feelings and emotions for them. When you add in the WOW, you'll elevate those emotions. And when that happens, people become storytellers for your brand because they'll need to share their experiences with others. And in this age of technology, the word "share" can become powerful for your brand because many more people can hear and read your story.

I'm curious. When have you experienced the WOW factor as a customer? Or better yet, what have you done to deliver that WOW factor to a customer? And in either scenario, how did this make you feel?

If we want to cement the Power of Hospitality, throw in some WOW every once in a while, and watch what happens.

BLACK TIE TAKEAWAY

Do you have a WOW budget in your organization? If not, can you create one? The money you spend will go a long way to creating loyal customers.

_____

_____

_____

_____

⊶ HOSPITALITY IS...

17

Knowing the balance between hi-tech and hi-touch.

Today, can you find a balance between your phone and your heart? I believe we have to. I'm all about hi-tech, and I know it will continue to evolve. Robots are starting to show up to serve people, and apps are taking the place of a human voice on the other end.

Maybe I'm old school, but while all of this is good, I still want to be able to talk to or email an actual person, not a bot. That's why finding a balance between hi-tech and hi-touch (coming from the heart) is more important today than ever.

Here's a story I was privileged to witness that shows the perfect balance of combining hi-tech and hi-touch.

I was flying to Memphis to speak at an association event, and towards the end of the flight, the senior flight attendant was walking up the aisle and stopped at the row directly in front of me. He was holding his Smartphone in one hand and looked to be on a mission. He came up to the passenger in 15B, greeted him by his name, and proceeded to thank him for being a Frequent Flyer member. How did he know this? In his hand was the "convenience," the data in his Smartphone. This data showed him the information he needed—name, where the passenger was sitting, and his Frequent Flyer status. He could have easily sent him an email or even a text to say "Thank you." But he decided to use the Power of Hospitality and make a personal connection. By doing this and thanking him, he left a memorable impression on the passenger and his wife. How do I know this? After the attendant left him, he turned to his wife and said, "That's never happened to me before. That was classy."

Later, I asked Pedro, the flight attendant, what that was all about. What he did was something simple but heartfelt. He took the time to make that personal/emotional connection while utilizing the technology that almost all of us now have at our fingertips.

He mentioned to me that it's all about connecting with his customers and thanking them for flying with his airline. He told me, "They're paying my salary, and I want to let them know how much I appreciate their business."

I couldn't have said it better myself, Pedro. Thank you for understanding what the Power of Hospitality is all about.

BLACK TIE TAKEAWAY

How are you combining the ever-changing power of "hi-tech" (convenience) with the power of hi-touch (making those personal connections) to create those lasting impressions?

_____

_____

_____

_____

⊛ HOSPITALITY IS...

18

Practicing active listening with your customers.

Can you believe one of my ideas to show hospitality is *actually* to keep your mouth closed? There's a difference between hearing and listening. I remember a few of my teachers in grade school asking us, "I know you can hear me, but are you really listening?"

To take it one step further, I believe when you practice active listening, you're genuinely showing Hospitality. How? Actively Listening means you're being focused and present on what your client or prospect is saying to you. You're not multi-tasking, not constantly looking at your phone to see who's trying to contact you. No, you're present and making that personal connection with them, all by listening. And you're asking those right questions and taking note of what they're telling you.

We can learn so much about our clients by just listening—to their real needs, their pain points, what they're trying to accomplish, and even some more personal facts (such as family, favorite hobby, or snack).

I've had to practice active listening. There were times I was formulating the thought I wanted to say to the person across the table from me, (or on the phone), and I wasn't paying attention to them. I missed a few of their points because while I heard *the words*, I just wasn't listening.

Here's the other key to active listening: We're telling our customers what they say matters to us and they're being heard. This concept is critical, especially when they have a challenge or are upset with your organization. Letting them know you're actually listening and will be able to help them is so important to them.

We taught our people to paraphrase and repeat back to our customers the point they were making or the challenge they were having with our company. Our people actively listened and—more importantly—told our customers we truly cared about their challenges and issues.

BLACK TIE TAKEAWAY

Put down your phone, lean in when people are talking, look them right in the eyes, and focus. Focus on them and what you're hearing them say. That's what active listening is all about.

_____

_____

_____

_____

⊶ HOSPITALITY IS...

19

Being the best or being the favorite.

··

If you were given the choice, would you strive to be the best in your industry or the favorite in it?

That answer is a little complicated because it involves both concepts I mentioned: being the best and being the favorite.

I believe we should strive to *be* the best, *do* our best every day, and make sure the people who work in our organizations also strive to do their best.

But when it comes to our customers, I think the word "best" is an opinion. It's tough to quantify that, isn't it? We are the "best" in the city, county, state, or country. Says who? It's like asking someone, "What's the best ice cream flavor?" There's no one answer; you're simply getting someone's opinion.

But to be someone's favorite in their minds—that's something special. That means you're taking care of them and their needs, going "Black Tie" to make their experiences special, and creating memories and stories for them they can tell others. You're going "Black Tie," so when someone asks them, "What's your favorite _____ ?" they'll naturally think of you.

Now, I will say sometimes your customer may get the question, "What's the best _____ around?" In their mind though, the word "favorite" still comes up because they'll naturally think of you and how you've been taking great care of them. And usually, they'll add a story or two to this conversation. This only affirms their answer.

Danny Meyer, the famed restaurateur who owns Union Square Hospitality, says, "To rule your market, you don't have to be the best at everything, you just need to be their favorite."

BLACK TIE TAKEAWAY

What steps are you taking to become the favorite in your customers' minds?

_____

_____

_____

_____

_____

HOSPITALITY IS...

20

Being Genuine, Sincere, and Thoughtful.

These are three fantastic traits to have and show to all our customers both external and internal. If you do, I promise you'll always have a job in whatever industry you're in now or aspire to work in.

If you remember from one of my previous chapters, Hospitality is about welcoming strangers. Being genuine, sincere, and thoughtful are three wonderful ways to start that. I know this can be challenging, and treating customers well doesn't seem to be getting any easier. That's not right, nor is it fair.

One of my goals as a CEO and leader was to work hard at these three important traits every day because you never knew who was watching. Case in point:

When I had my events/catering company, we always had pre-event meetings for the staff who worked on each event. This was the time to go over the event details and give them some insights into the clients.

This particular event was a wedding. I sincerely enjoyed getting to know the couple and working with them every step to plan their special event. I mentioned this to my staff at that meeting that day, and I was sincere about everything I said about the bride and groom because I had developed a fondness for them through the entire process. I ended my meeting by telling the staff that while every event we do is significant, this one for me was extra special because of the bride and groom, and I wanted to make sure that all of us were going to be at the top of our games that night.

About 10 minutes after the meeting ended, I said hello to the bride's parents, as I had gotten to know them a little as well. The bride's mother asked if I had met their son, and I hadn't yet.

As we shook hands, he said, "I already know who you are."

This surprised me because I had never met him, and I wondered what he was going to say.

He then said, "I heard you talking to your staff at your meeting about the wedding and the wonderful things you had to say about my sister and her new husband. And I want to tell you that was one of the classiest things anyone has ever done. I could tell by your words and your tone how genuine and sincere you were with those comments. And I was ready to run through a brick wall for you when you closed your meeting with your last request to your staff. Thank you, and I already know this is going to be a day that she and my family will never forget."

I was shocked and humbled by those words because I had no idea he was there and had overheard our meeting. But the impact of those words was priceless for him. And I was just being myself. But my words also inspired my staff because what I did became contagious, and they wanted to work and serve at their highest level.

BLACK TIE TAKEAWAY

Aspire to put into practice these three traits in front of every customer: being genuine, sincere, and thoughtful. You never know who's watching you these days.

_____

_____

_____

_____

(⊶) HOSPITALITY IS...

21

Part of Customer Service 101—except it's not 101 any longer.

Coming out of the pandemic, I had more than one colleague tell me, "Bob, it seems like people have forgotten the basics of Customer Service." And while I understand their thoughts, it's been challenging for both organizations and people to take care of their customers with so many other distractions. No matter what, though, people are choosing to spend their money on a product or service, and they want to be taken care of in a timely and friendly matter.

So why are we feeling this way, and what are those "back-to-the-basic" qualities we need to revisit? Yes, the distractions are real for companies and their people. Some of them are understaffed and overworked. And it can be hard to keep up. However, I think the following four traits are missing in some instances. How do we fix this? As hard as it seems to pull off, it boils down to training, mentoring, and coaching.

1. Communication

It's frustrating for customers to be bounced around because no one in the company is communicating with each other. And with all the technology we have at our fingertips today, companies need to find a way to train people to talk to each other. This means employees need to leave their silos, be proactive, and talk. However, what they want to do will work for the customer too.

2. Listening

I discussed listening in a previous chapter, but the ideas bear repeating. Sometimes organizations follow "their book" in all situations. This magical book has all the answers to any customer's questions—except when it doesn't. Employees focus so much on what's in "the book" that they fail to actively listen to what the customer is trying to explain to them.

3. Empathy

This one is a two-way street. Both the employees and their customers need to get back to this one. One way to do this is to put yourself in other's shoes. As a customer, what's it like to be that employee who is working their 3rd long shift in a row because people keep calling off or not showing up? How would you want to be treated by a customer if you were in their shoes?

And as an employee, what do your body language, actions, and words look and sound like to the customer? Can you imagine what their day has been like, and now they're waiting for a long time without any recognition or action from you?

We all need to be more empathic. Yes, it's easier said than done, but we can do it.

4. Follow up

We're getting busy, and we sometimes forget to follow up. But why? If you're an employee, and someone contacts you to get more information about your services or would like to give you their business, why isn't there a follow-up?

I realized early in my career to underpromise and overdeliver. We've all heard this saying, correct? So why is it the exact opposite in many situations today?

The hospitable thing to do is to follow up when you say you will, even if you don't have the answer yet because the customer can be frustrated if no information is coming back. But just like empathy, I believe this one is a two-way street.

If you're a customer or prospect, can you give the courtesy to the organization of either telling them yes or no? I agree that no one likes to be told, "No, I don't want your product or service." It's just a part of doing business.

And this way, it helps the organization move on as well. Look around your organization and see if you need to "shake off the rust" from these concepts. This will help your Customer Service 101.

BLACK TIE TAKEAWAY

What are the Customer Service basics you believe your organization needs to get back to? If you're unsure, ask some of your best customers. They will help you.

_____

_____

_____

_____

⬤ HOSPITALITY IS...

22

Knowing the second impression is just as powerful as the first one.

I had the incredible fortune of meeting future Hall of Famers while we worked at the Pro Football Hall of Fame. And as you read earlier, one of the true highlights of our business was the opportunity to cater 25 of the Hall of Fame Induction Parties. As the owner of my company, I was able to meet almost all of these individuals as well as other Hall of Famers and NFL players.

One player made an impression on me; in fact, I met him at the first party we catered in 2006. I had the privilege of meeting and working with Harry Carson Jr. of the New York Giants. Harry was an incredible football player, but more importantly, he was an incredible human being. He was genuine and humble from the first time I met with him to talk about his party. I'll always remember that, but I'll never forget two other details about Harry.

1. My son, who was nine at the time of Harry's induction party, got to meet him. Adam paid a quick visit to the event, and I asked him if he would like to meet Harry. He had no idea who Harry was, except that he was a football player, and to a nine-year-old, he was huge! As you may imagine, the party for the Hall of Famers is a pretty big deal—a whirlwind of an evening for them, as they were inundated with family, friends, and colleagues wanting to talk to them. As I came up to Harry to ask him if he needed anything to drink, he saw this "little guy" dressed in a chef coat right next to me. He stopped what he was doing, bent over to ask Adam his name, and proceeded to shake Adam's hand. He then talked to my son for the next two minutes. I never asked Harry if he could talk to my son, but Harry recognized that opportunity to meet Adam and thank him for coming to his party! Adam still talks about that to this day. Why? Harry made him *feel special* for those two minutes.

2. Fast forward three years later, and we're catering five of the Hall of Fame Induction events in one evening. I'm moving around to each of these events, making sure everything is running smoothly. As I walk to one of the air-conditioned tents, a golf cart slows down next to me, and the passenger in the cart turns to say, "It's Bob, right? You catered my Hall of Fame party three years ago." It was Harry Carson Jr. "I know you're busy, but I wanted to say hello and let you know that my people are still talking about my

party. Thanks again!" Again, the conversation was two minutes, but what an impression Harry made on me. I've forgotten several things about that night and the parties we catered, but I'll never forget the second impression he made on me three years later.

BLACK TIE TAKEAWAY

Make the time to "make someone's day" by how you greet them and what you say to them. People don't usually forget when you put your attention on them.

_____

_____

_____

_____

HOSPITALITY IS...

23

Providing it even while customers are paying more for products and getting less service.

....

Yes, prices are going up on everything, and yes, there are staffing shortages everywhere. But does that mean the customer experience we provide needs to suffer? Apparently, in some organizations, this is the easy way out.

"Sorry, we can't help you. We're short-staffed because no one wants to work." I'm sure you've heard this line more than once from companies you try to do business with. And while a part of me gets it and empathizes with these companies, most of me doesn't.

If I have a question about a product or can't find it in the store, I still expect that staff person to treat me the right way. I expect them to help me or find someone who *will*, to show Hospitality—not brush me off because they're too busy or don't know the answer.

There are two grocery stores where I often shop. Both are medium-to-large chains. Store A is known for lower prices, and you've always needed to bag your groceries. There are no self-checkouts.

Store B has higher prices, more amenities, a handful of self-checkout registers, and people bagging your groceries for you. Even with everything that's happened because of COVID-19, Store A hasn't changed. Yes, prices have gone up, but a person still greets you, makes sure to ask if you were able to get everything you came in for, and scans and loads your groceries into a cart at record-breaking speed. Watching this is amazing. If three or more people are waiting in a checkout line, suddenly, another staff person magically appears from somewhere in the store to open up another register to check out more shoppers. That's providing more service and Hospitality.

Store B did the opposite. It decided to take most of its staffed checkout registers and turn them into self-checkout. On a recent shopping trip, I counted 19 available registers, yet only two had an actual person ready to help check customers out. And another staff person was there too, but they weren't on the extra registers.

I even asked one of the staff why there were so many self-checkout registers. The answer was predictable to me. "We can't find anyone to work, so we've needed to cut back our services."

I'm thinking to myself, your prices have increased, which means I'm paying more for your products, and now I have to do all the work to purchase your products, even if I have a cart full of groceries. And I noticed many people who had many items in their carts. It was going to take them at least 5-7 minutes to scan and bag their groceries.

To me, this isn't Hospitality.

What's Store A doing that Store B isn't? They're still making their customers feel valued because they're keeping a close eye on the customer experience they're delivering. They're not the flashiest store, nor do they have a lot of choices on some brands, but they make up for that with the Hospitality they're continually showing their customers.

What does that mean for me? I'm getting most of our groceries at Store A and only go to Store B for that handful of items that aren't available at Store A.

BLACK TIE TAKEAWAY

How do you create and show Hospitality, even when times are a little tough?
Remember, this starts and stops with your people—how you treat them and how they treat your customers.

_____

_____

_____

🎀 HOSPITALITY IS...

24

Striving to become "Rememorable."

....

I'm going to make up a word for this chapter. I checked because it's not in the dictionary, but I think using it can be powerful when moving your customers to the Brand Ambassador stage where you can see an increase in engagement, loyalty, retention—and revenue.

"Rememorable." You mean "Memorable," right, Bob?

No, it's being *Rememorable*. You see, I think if you're a company, product, service, or individual who is *rememorable* in a customer's mind, you've done something (or several things) your customers remember. If they're remembering your brand, this means they're feeling good about the experience(s) they're having with you. Once this happens, the opportunities for them to become storytellers for your brand increase because they want to tell people what you've done to make them *feel* this way. You're in their memory. When someone asks, "Who do you recommend?" or "Who's your favorite?" your company becomes rememorable to them.

How do you become rememorable? You could start by reviewing each of the previous chapters. Each contains an action you can perform to create an opportunity to make your customers, employees, and community members more valued, appreciated, welcomed, and loved. Then look for ways to implement them. Make it a point of always looking for ways to take Hospitality to the "Black Tie" level. And I believe this is another key: Don't boast about it. Let your actions and your words speak for you. Trust me. Word will get around about what's happening. There are reasons why some brands you haven't heard of have a line of people out their door waiting for them to open a new store or launch a new product. I believe part of this is becoming rememorable in their customers' minds and then letting them do the talking and storytelling. Try it. It just may work for you.

BLACK TIE TAKEAWAY

What are you doing to become Rememorable in your customers' minds? What will they remember about your brand, their experience with your brand, and their journey with you?

(⊶) **HOSPITALITY** IS...

25

Turning your customers into Brand Ambassadors.

I know I've enjoyed putting together these hospitality principles, and I hope they make a difference in how to go about not only serving your customers, co-workers, and prospects but also in what you're doing to create experiences for potential returning customers.

Once that happens, you've achieved that coveted loyal customer, that Brand Ambassador. What's that? Here's my definition: someone who can't wait to tell others how you've made them feel. Everything I've talked about in the previous chapters culminates with this. I believe there are two types of these Ambassadors. We always think of the obvious one—our customers. The second is just as valuable, if not more—your employees. Brand Ambassadors are the key to the long-term success of your organization. Why? The more retention and engagement you have, the more revenue and profit your organization should have.

Without them, you'll need to replenish your clients and employees. A recent study by the Temkin Group backs this up. They concluded that your loyal customers (Brand Ambassadors) are:

- Five times more likely to repurchase from you.
- Four times more likely to refer you.
- Seven times more likely to try something new from you.

Yes, every customer and employee is important to you, but can you see what the power of being a Brand Ambassador can do for your organization?

I believe it starts and stops with Hospitality.

BLACK TIE TAKEAWAY

Jot down 5 of your Brand Ambassadors. Why are they Ambassadors for you? How long have they been one? What can you do to keep them in this role?

About
the Author

BOB PACANOVSKY

Bob Pacanovsky never thought he would be an entrepreneur. But looking back, he realized this journey started when he worked for his uncle's Italian restaurant, where he learned how to take care of customers and make them loyal in an extremely competitive industry.

Fast forward about ten years, and Bob couldn't find a quality pizza to order. With a degree in finance and a background in marketing and advertising, he did the only logical thing: He called his uncle, tweaked the recipes a bit, and started making pizzas at home (okay, maybe not that logical). The pizzas went over so well that he and his wife opened their first Italian restaurant in 1994. This started his 30-year journey as an entrepreneur, primarily in the hospitality industry.

Bob owned two restaurants: one that worked, and one that didn't. And it was here that he started putting his customer service ideas into place. He quickly got a loyal following of customers, some of whom would drive more than 30 minutes for the food and experience. Then, Bob learned a valuable lesson in customer service and leadership, as the second restaurant he opened only lasted 13 months before it closed.

While he owned the restaurants, he discovered catering. Not wanting to be deterred, he took his first restaurant and turned it into an off-site catering company. This started a journey in the events and catering industry where his company grew in 15 years from a two-person operation to a company that employed over 50 people; worked at over 60 unique venues throughout Northeast ohio; and created over 7,000 meetings, events, meetings, and receptions (including catering 25 Pro Football Hall of Fame Induction Events over five years).

During this time, Bob created a comprehensive training program for all his employees that focused on creating a WOW experience and a lasting impression. This program concentrated on three concepts vital to the success of the company: establishing a solid workplace culture, developing his people into leaders, and creating a consistent and memorable customer experience.

Bob sold his company at the end of 2014 and started his journey as a professional speaker. He has achieved Professional Member status of the National Speakers Association and has spoken throughout the United States to numerous associations, companies, and organizations.

He is most proud of being married to his wife, Connie, for 32 years and his son, Adam, an entrepreneur in Los Angeles.

How I Can Help You

People most often ask me, "What do you speak and train on?"

Every organization has *some* people who get what it means to deliver a consistent, top-notch, "Black Tie" Customer Service Experience, but *everyone* in an organization needs to understand this. I turn every member of the organization into those people who get it. Think about how much loyalty, retention, and revenue your organization could generate if every employee operated at that level!

If your organization or association is ready for an opportunity like this, let's talk!

I offer customized keynotes, workshops, and trainings on Customer Experience & Hospitality, Selfless Leadership & Employee Engagement and Retention.

Turn the page for my contact information!

Contact me at:

Bob@BobPacanovsky.com or (330) 352-6084

Find me and follow me on social media:

- Linkedin.com/in/Bob-Pacanovsky
- Facebook.com/BobPacanovskyBlackTie
- Instagram.com/black_tie_experience/

Website:

www.BobPacanovsky.com

Made in the USA
Middletown, DE
26 November 2024